♫♫ \ Can Sing ♫♫ en français!

Fun Songs for Learning French

Louise Morgan-Williams & Gaëtane Armbrust
Designed and Illustrated by Jane Launchbury
Edited by Sue Hook
Music for original songs by Ed Montgignan

Contents

Published by Passport Books,
a division of NTC/Contemporary Publishing Group, Inc.,
4255 West Touhy Avenue,
Lincolnwood (Chicago), Illinois 60712-1975 U.S.A.
© 1994 by NTC/Contemporary Publishing Group, Inc.
All rights reserved. No part of this book may be reproduced, stored
in a retrieval system, or transmitted in any form or by any means,
electronic, mechanical, photocopying, recording, or otherwise, without
prior written permission of NTC/Contemporary Publishing Group, Inc.
Printed in Hong Kong.
International Standard Book Number: 0-8442-1457-4

0 1 2 3 4 5 6 7 8 9 WKT 9 8 7 6 5

About This Book

From a very early age, children respond to the rhythms and sounds of the language they hear around them. They have an amazing ability to mimic sounds and to acquire language easily, an ability that diminishes as they grow older.

Action songs and rhymes play an important role in language learning at this early stage. They help stimulate awareness and interest in language, and provide an enjoyable means of playing with sounds and exploring words.

In **I Can Sing *en français!*** songs have been carefully selected to appeal to children. The collection includes both original songs that incorporate familiar, everyday themes and traditional songs loved by generations of children all over the world. On the cassette available with this book, the songs are sung by boys and girls who are native speakers of French.

Each song text is accompanied by a simple music score for children and adults who want to play the songs themselves. The illustrations help children associate the French words with the action and story of the song.

Under each French word illustrated on the vocabulary pages is a pronunciation key to help in saying the word correctly. (There is more help with pronunciation below.) Say the words together, and then see if the child can pick out those words when you listen to the songs on the cassette available with this book. You'll also see the English translation under each vocabulary word. Full English translations of the song texts appear on pages 31 and 32.

As children sing these songs, they will start to become familiar with simple language structures. For example, nouns in French are either masculine or feminine. To help children begin associating the correct gender with the nouns, we have placed a boy or girl symbol beside each of these words illustrated in the book. This will give children a headstart as they move on to the next stage of learning.

We hope children enjoy these first steps **en français!**   Louise Morgan Williams   J. Humbert

---

USING THE PRONUNCIATION GUIDE

If you follow the pronunciation guides in the book and listen to the cassette, you will see and hear how the French words should sound. Some of the sounds call for special explanation, however:

oo(r)	like the <u>-our</u> in "tour," e.g., **cour, tours**		*zj*	like the <u>-s-</u> in "measure," e.g., **je, neige**
uh	like the <u>a-</u> in "about," e.g., **je, regarde, renard**		*ew*	like the <u>-ew</u> in "pew," e.g., **ruche, une, perdu**
euh	like the <u>-oo-</u> in "wood," eg., **deux, bleu**			
a(n)	like the <u>-an-</u> in "sang" without the "g" sound at the end, e.g., **main, un**			
aw(n)	like the <u>-on-</u> in "song" without the "g" sound at the end, e.g., **planter, vent**			
o(n)	like the <u>-on-</u> in "phone" with the "n" sound barely pronounced, e.g., **rond, son**			

2

Quand Trois Poules

poules †
pool
hens

champs †
shaw(n)
fields

Quand trois poules vont aux champs,
La première va devant.
La seconde suit la première,
La troisième vient la dernière.
Quand trois poules vont aux champs,
La première va devant.

troisième †
trwah-zi-em
third

dernière †
dair-ni-yair
last

première †
pruh-mi-yair
first

seconde †
s'go(n)d
second

devant
d'vaw(n)
in front

trois
trwah
three

3

Comptons

Un, deux, trois, quatre, cinq;
Comme les doigts de ma main.

Un, deux, trois; un, deux, trois;
Voilà Papa, Maman et moi.   (refrain)

Un, deux, trois, quatre; un, deux. trois, quatre;
Avec ma petite soeur, Héléna.   (refrain)

Un, deux, trois, quatre, cinq; un, deux, trois, quatre, cinq;
Si on compte mon petit chat.

Un, deux, trois, quatre, cinq; un, deux, trois, quatre, cinq;
C'est comme les cinq doigts de ma main!

comptons
co(n)-to(n)
let's count

un	**deux**	**trois**	**quatre**	**cinq**
a(n)	*deuh*	*trwah*	*ka-tr*	*sa(n)k*
one	two	three	four	five

moi
mwah
me

papa ♂
pah-pah
dad

maman ♀
mah-maw(n)
mom

petit
p'tee
little

doigts ♂
dwah
fingers

petite
p'teet
little

main ♀
ma(n)
hand

soeur ♀
sur
sister

chat ♂
shah
cat

5

Tu Entends...?

Tu entends l'oiseau
Qui est dans le nid ?
L'oiseau fait "cui, cui, cui!"

Tu entends l'abeille
Qui est dans la ruche?
L'abeille fait "bzzz, bzzz, bzzz!"

Tu entends le chat
Qui est dans l'arbre?
Le chat fait "miaou, miaou, miaou!"

Tu entends le chien
Qui est dans la niche?
Le chien fait "ouah, ouah, ouah!"

Tu entends la vache
Qui est dans le pré?
La vache fait "meuh, meuh, meuh!"

Tu entends la poule
Qui est dans la cour?
La poule fait "cot, cot, cot!"

Tu entends le poisson
Qui est dans la mer?
Le poisson fait "flic, flac, floc!"

Tu Entends...?

tu   entends
tew aw(n)-taw(n)
you hear

oiseau †
wah-zoh
bird

dans
daw(n)
in

nid †
nee
nest

abeille ⚥
ah-bay
bee

ruche †
rewsh
hive

chat †
shah
cat

arbre †
ahr-br
tree

chien ✝
shee-a(n)
dog

niche ✝
neesh
kennel

vache ✝
vahsh
cow

pré ✝
pray
meadow

cour ✝
coor
yard

poule ✝
pool
hen

poisson ✝
pwah-so(n)
fish

mer ✝
mair
sea

9

Bon Appétit!

bon appétit
bo(n) ah-pay-tee
good appetite

qui veut
kee veuh
who wants

Qui veut un croissant?
Non, merci, non pas pour moi.

Qui veut une orange?
Non, merci, non pas pour moi.

Qui veut un sandwich?
Non, merci, non pas pour moi.

Qui veut une banane?
Non, merci, non pas pour moi.

Qui veut des bonbons?
Oui, s'il te plaît, moi, moi, moi!

1 un
a(n)
a

croissant †
krwah-saw(n)
croissant

1
une
ewn
an

orange ✝
o-raw(n)zj
orange

sandwich ✝
saw(n)-dweetsh
sandwich

banane ✝
bah-nahn
banana

non   merci
no(n)   mair-see
no   thank you

pas pour moi
pah-poor-mwah
not for me

bonbons ✝
bo(n)-bo(n)
candy

oui   s'il te plaît
wee   seel-tuh-play
yes   please

11

Tourne En Rond

Je me brosse les dents,
Je me peigne les cheveux,
Je me lave les mains
Et je tourne, tourne, tourne en rond.

Je mets mon manteau,
Je prends mon bonnet,
Je sors mon écharpe
Et je tourne, tourne, tourne en rond.

tourne **en rond**
toorn *aw(n)-ro(n)*
turn round

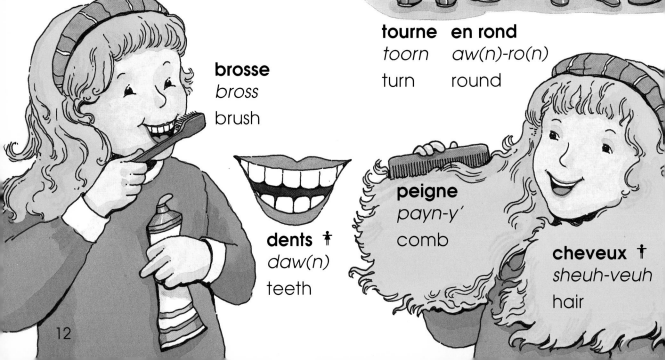

brosse
bross
brush

dents ✝
daw(n)
teeth

peigne
payn-y′
comb

cheveux ✝
sheuh-veuh
hair

12

lave
lahv
wash

mains ✝
ma(n)
hands

mets
may
put on

manteau ✝
maw(n)-toh
coat

sors
sor
take out

bonnet ✝
bun-nay
hat

prends
praw(n)
take

écharpe ✝
ay-shahrp
scarf

13

14

Savez-Vous Planter Les Choux?

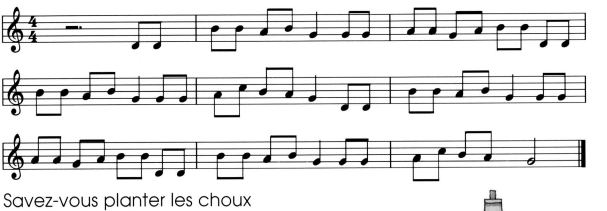

Savez-vous planter les choux
A la mode, à la mode,
Savez-vous planter les choux
A la mode de chez nous ?

On les plante avec la main
A la mode, à la mode,
On les plante avec la main
A la mode de chez nous.

Savez-vous planter les choux ....

On les plante avec le coude, etc.

On les plante avec la tête, etc.

On les plante avec le nez, etc.

Savez-Vous Planter Les Choux?

choux ✝
shoo
cabbages

planter
plaw(n)-tay
plant

main ✝
ma(n)
hand

coude ✝
cood
elbow

Le Temps

Regarde le soleil.
Il brille dans le ciel.

Regarde la pluie.
Elle glisse sur le toit.

Regarde la neige.
Elle tombe sur la ville.

Regarde le vent.
Il souffle dans le bois.

pluie †
plwee
rain

glisse
gleece
slides off

sur
sewr
on

toit †
twah
roof

neige †
nezj
snow

tombe
to(n)b
falls

ville †
veel
town

vent †
vaw(n)
wind

souffle
soo-fl
blows

dans
daw(n)
in

bois †
bwah
wood

J'ai Perdu Ma Poupée Bleue

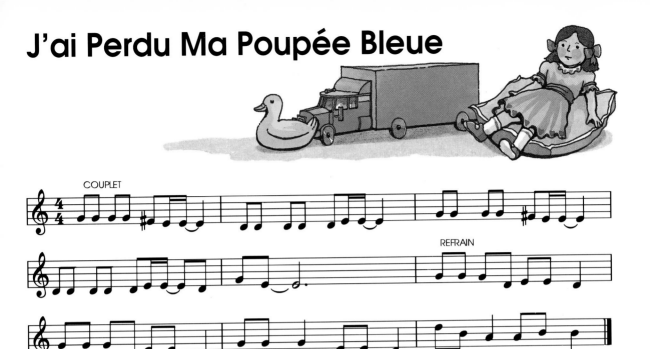

COUPLET

REFRAIN

J'ai perdu ma poupée bleue,
J'ai perdu mon bateau rouge.
Je les aimais tous les deux,
Je les aimais tous les deux.

J'ai trouvé ma poupée bleue,
J'ai trouvé mon bateau rouge.
Je les aime tous les deux,
Je les aime tous les deux.

J'ai perdu ma toupie bleue,
J'ai perdu mon canard jaune.
Je les aimais tous les deux,
Je les aimais tous les deux.

J'ai trouvé ma toupie bleue,
J'ai trouvé mon canard jaune.
Je les aime tous les deux,
Je les aime tous les deux.

J'ai perdu ma trompette bleue,
J'ai perdu mon camion vert.
Je les aimais tous les deux,
Je les aimais tous les deux.

J'ai trouvé ma trompette bleue,
J'ai trouvé mon camion vert.
Je les aime tous les deux,
Je les aime tous les deux.

J'ai Perdu Ma Poupée Bleue

perdu
pair-dew
lost

poupée ✝
poo-pay
doll

bleue
bleuh
blue

bateau ✝
bah-toh
boat

rouge
roozj
red

aime
em
love

tous les deux
too-lay-deuh
both

trouvé
troo-vay
found

canard ✝
cah-nahr
duck

jaune
zjohn
yellow

camion ✝
cah-mee-o(n)
truck

toupie ✝
too-pee
top

trompette ✝
tro(n)-pet
trumpet

vert
vair
green

23

Le Renard Malin

Petit poussin, bonjour!
Ah, tu vas faire un tour.
Mais, fais attention à toi!

Rentre vite où tu habites,
Car je vois au loin
Le renard malin!

petit
p'tee
little

poussin †
poo-sa(n)
chick

bonjour
bo(n)-zjoor
hello

rentre
raw(n)-tr
go back

vite
veet
quickly

où tu habites
oo-tew-ah-beet
where you live

renard †
ruh-nahr
fox

je   vois
zjuh   vwah
I   see

au loin
oh lwa(n)
in the distance

Petit lapin, bonjour!
Ah, tu vas faire un tour.
Mais, fais attention à toi!

Rentre vite où tu habites,
Car je vois au loin
Le renard malin!

malin
mah-la(n)
cunning

lapin †
lah-pa(n)
rabbit

Quand Je Serai Grand

Quand je serai grand, je serai pilote.
Quand je serai grand, je serai chanteur.
Quand je serai grand, je serai pompier.
Non, non, non, non, non, non,
Je serai comme Papa.

Quand je serai grande, je serai docteur.
Quand je serai grande, je serai actrice.
Quand je serai grande, je serai danseuse.
Non, non, non, non, non, non,
Je serai comme Maman.

Quand Je Serai Grand

grand
graw(n)
big

pilote †
pee-lot
pilot

chanteur †
shaw(n)-tur
singer

non
no(n)
no

papa †
pah-pah
dad

pompier †
po(n)-pee-ay
fireman

grande †
graw(n)d
big

docteur †
dok-tur
doctor

actrice †
ak-treece
actress

danseuse †
daw(n)-seuhz
dancer

maman †
mah-maw(n)
mom

Les Petites Marionettes

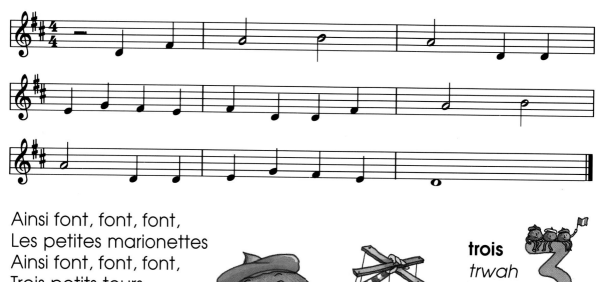

Ainsi font, font, font,
Les petites marionettes
Ainsi font, font, font,
Trois petits tours
Et puis s'en vont.

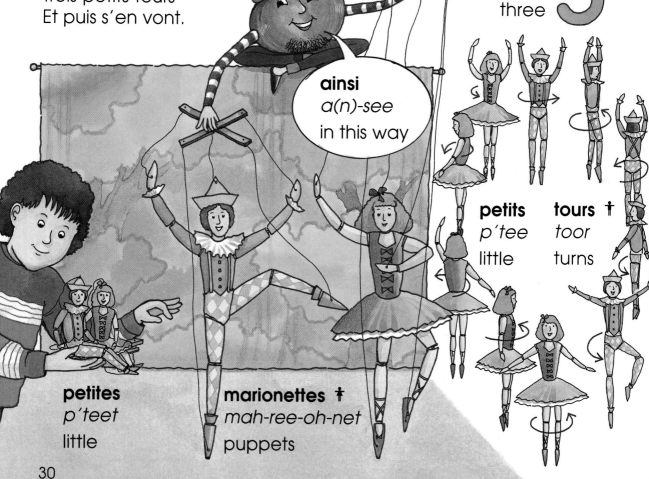

ainsi
a(n)-see
in this way

trois
trwah
three

petits
p'tee
little

tours †
toor
turns

petites
p'teet
little

marionettes †
mah-ree-oh-net
puppets

Translations

Quand Trois Poules ...
When Three Hens ...

When three hens go off to the fields,
The first one goes in front.
The second one follows the first,
The third one comes last.
When three hens go off to the fields,
The first one goes in front.

Comptons
Let's Count

One, two three, four, five;
It's like the fingers of my hand.

One, two, three; one, two, three;
Here is Dad, Mom and me.   (refrain)

One, two, three, four; one, two, three, four;
With my little sister, Helena.   (refrain)

One, two, three, four, five;
One, two, three, four, five;
If you count my little cat.

One, two, three, four, five;
One, two, three, four, five;
It's like the five fingers of my hand.

Tu Entends ...?
Can You Hear ...?

Can you hear the bird
That is in the nest?
The bird goes "tweet, tweet, tweet!"

Can you hear the bee
That is in the hive?
The bee goes "bzzz, bzzz, bzzz!"

Can you hear the cat
That is in the tree?
The cat goes "miaow, miaow, miaow!"

Can you hear the dog
That is in the kennel?
The dog goes "woof, woof, woof!"

Can you hear the cow
That is in the meadow?
The cow goes "moo, moo, moo!"

Can you hear the hen
That is in the farmyard?
The hen goes "cluck, cluck, cluck!"

Can you hear the fish
That is in the sea?
The fish goes "*splash, splash, splash!*"

Bon Appétit
Enjoy Your Food

Who would like a croissant?
No, thank you, no, not for me.

Who would like an orange?
No, thank you, no, not for me.

Who would like a sandwich?
No, thank you, no, not for me.

Who would like a banana?
No, thank you, no, not for me.

Who would like some candy?
Yes, please, me, me, me!

Tourne En Rond
Turn Around

I brush my teeth,
I comb my hair,
I wash my hands
And I turn, turn, turn around.

I put on my coat,
I take my hat,
I fetch my scarf
And I turn, turn, turn around.

Savez-Vous Planter Les Choux?
Do You Know How To Plant Cabbages?

Do you know how to plant cabbages
Like we do it, like we do it,
Do you know how to plant cabbages
Like we do it at home?

You plant them with your hand
Like we do it, like we do it,
You plant them with your hand
Like we do it at home.

Do you know how to plant cabbages .....

You plant them with your elbow, etc .....

You plant them with your head, etc .....

You plant them with your nose, etc .....

Le Temps
The Weather

Look at the sun.
It's shining in the sky.

Look at the rain.
It's sliding off the roof.

Look at the snow.
It's falling on the town.

Look at the wind.
It's blowing through the trees.

J'ai Perdu Ma Poupée Bleue
I've Lost My Blue Doll

I've lost my blue doll,
I've lost my red boat.
I loved them both,
I loved them both.

I've found my blue doll,
I've found my red boat.
I love them both,
I love them both.

I've lost my blue top,
I've lost my yellow duck.
I loved them both,
I loved them both.

I've found my blue top,
I've found my yellow duck.
I love them both,
I love them both.

I've lost my blue trumpet,
I've lost my green truck.
I loved them both,
I loved them both.

I've found my blue trumpet,
I've found my green truck.
I love them both.
I love them both.

Le Renard Malin
The Cunning Fox

Little chick, hello!
Ah, you're going for a little walk,
But, take care!

Go home quickly,
Because I can see in the distance
The cunning fox!

Little rabbit, (repeat as above)

Quand Je Serai Grand
When I Grow Up

When I grow up, I want to be a pilot.
When I grow up, I want to be a singer.
When I grow up, I want to be a fireman.
No, no, no, no, no, no,
I want to be just like my Dad.

When I grow up, I want to be a doctor.
When I grow up, I want to be an actress.
When I grow up, I want to be a dancer.
No, no, no, no, no, no,
I want to be just like my Mom.

Les Petites Marionettes
The Little Puppets

This is the way,
This is the way,
The little string puppets
Do three little turns
And then go away.

With our thanks to the children
who sang these songs:
**Amaya, Aurélie, Célina, Claire,
Flora, Nicolas, Oriana, Virginia,
Guido.**